PRESCRIPTION
FOR A TIRED HOUSEWIFE

Prescription for a Tired Housewife

● ● ●

A Tyndale Treasure by
DR. JAMES DOBSON

Tyndale House
Publishers, Inc.
Wheaton, Illinois

Prescription for a Tired Housewife is adapted
from What Wives Wish Their Husbands Knew
about Women by Dr. James Dobson, copyright © 1975
by Tyndale House Publishers, Inc.,
Wheaton, Illinois

Library of Congress Catalog Card Number 75-39879
ISBN 0-8423-4878-6
Fifth printing, December 1980
Printed in the United States of America.

FATIGUE AND TIME PRESSURE

Flip Wilson once said, "If I had my entire life to live over, I doubt if I'd have the strength." There must be many women who agree with him, for *"fatigue and time pressure"* ranked as the second most frequent cause for depression among women who completed a questionnaire I devised about emotional problems. As I have journeyed across the United States, from the metropolitan centers to the farms of Iowa, I have found extremely busy people running faster and faster down the road to exhaustion. We have become a nation of huffers and puffers, racing through the day and moonlighting into the night. Even our recreation is marked by this breakneck pace.

How frequently does your head whirl and spin with the obligations of an impossible "to do" list? "I simply must get the bills paid this morning and the grocery shopping can't wait another day. And my children! I've had so little time to be with them lately that we hardly seem like a family anymore. Maybe I can read them a story tonight. And I mustn't neglect my own body; exercise is important and I've got to find time for that. Perhaps I could

1

'Jump Along with Jack' on television each morning. My annual physical is overdue, too. And I ought to be reading more. Everyone knows that it's important to keep your mind active, so I just shouldn't neglect the printed page. If I could get into bed an hour earlier each night I could do plenty of reading. And we really should be taking more time to maintain our spiritual lives. That's one area we cannot afford to neglect. And what about our social obligations? We can't expect to have friends if we never get together. The Johnsons have had us over twice now, and I know they're waiting for us to reciprocate. We'll just have to set a date and keep it, that's all. And there are so many things that need fixing and repairing on the house. And the income tax is due next month . . . I'd better block out some time for that. And I . . . excuse me, the phone is ringing."

So we're too busy; everyone can see that. But what does a hectic pace have to do with depression? Just this: every obligation which we shirk is a source of guilt. When there are more commitments than we can possibly handle, then self-esteem is further damaged by each failure. "I'm really a lousy parent; I'm too exhausted to be a good wife; I'm disorganized and confused; I'm out of touch with the world around me and I don't have any real friends; even God is displeased with me." Truly, overextended lives contribute to emotional pathology in numerous ways. It was this source of frustration that the women reflected on my questionnaire.

Vince Lombardi, the late, great football coach for the Green Bay Packers, once gave an inspired speech to his team at the beginning of the fall season. His comments were recorded that day, and have considerable applicability to our theme at this point. Coach Lombardi was discussing the impact of exhaustion on human courage, and he made this brief statement: "Fatigue makes cowards of us all!" How right he was. Physical depletion renders us less able to cope with the noisiness of children, the dishwasher that won't work, and the thousands of other minor irritations of everyday living. It is also said, *when you are tired you are attacked by ideas you thought you had conquered long ago.* Perhaps this explains why women (and men) who are grossly overworked become cowards—whining, griping, and biting those whom they love the most.

If fatigue and time pressure produce such a strain, then why do we permit ourselves to become so busy? Well, for one thing, everyone apparently thinks his hectic pace is a temporary problem. I have heard all the reasons why "things are kind of tough right now." Here are the four most common for the young family:

1. Jerry just started this new business, you know, so it'll take a few years to get it going.

2. Well, Pete is in school for two more years, so I've been trying to work to help out with the finances.

3. We have a new baby in our house and you know what that means.

4. We just bought a new house, which we're fixing up ourselves.

To hear them tell it, there is a slower day coming, as soon as the present obligations are met. But you know it is an illusion. Their "temporary" pressures are usually sandwiched back to back with other temporary pressures, gradually developing into a long-term style of living. My secretary taped a little note to her typewriter which read, "As soon as the rush is over, I'm going to have a nervous breakdown. I've earned it, I deserve it, and nobody is going to keep me from having it." Time proves, however, that the rush is never over. As the Beatles said of women in their song "Lady Madonna," "See how they run!"

No one "runs" much faster than the mother of multiple preschool children. Not only is she rushed from morning to night, but she experiences an unusual kind of emotional stress as well. Youngsters between two and five years of age have an uncanny ability to unravel an adult nervous system. Maybe it is listening to the constant diarrhea of words that wears Mom down to utter exhaustion. Hasn't every mother in the world had the following "conversation" with her child at least a million times?

Johnny: Can I have a cookie, Mom? Huh, Mom? Can I? Can I have one, Mom? Why can't I have one? Huh? Huh, Mom? Can I? Mom? Mom, can I? Can I have a cookie now?

Mom: No, Johnny, it's too close to lunch time.

Johnny: Just one, Mom? Can't I have just one little cookie now? Huh? Can I? I will eat my lunch. Okay, Mom? Okay? I will eat all my lunch. Okay? Can I? Just one? Spotty would like one, too. Dogs like cookies,

too, don't they, Mom? Don't they? Don't
dogs like cookies, too?

Mom: Yes, Johnny. I guess dogs like cookies, too.

Johnny: Can Spotty and I have one? Huh? Can we?

Although "mom" began her day with a guarded
optimism about life, these questions have reduced
her to a lump of putty by 4 P.M.

My wife and I observed this process in action
while sitting in a restaurant in Hawaii last summer.
A young couple and their four-year-old son were
seated near us, and the child was rattling like a
machine gun. If he stopped even to breathe, I
couldn't detect it. Nonsensical questions and comments were bubbling forth from his inexhaustible
fountain of verbiage. It was easy to see the harass-
ment on his parents' faces, for they were about to
explode from the constant onslaught of noise.
Finally, the mother leaned over to her son and
without moving her lips she sent this unmistakable
message through her clenched teeth . . . one sylla-
ble at a time: "Shut! Up! Shut! Up! Don't—say—
one—more—word! If—you—say—one—more—
word—I—will—scream!" We had to smile, for her
frustration was vaguely familiar to us. This young
woman told us at the checkstand that her verbose
son had talked from morning to night for two years,
and her composure teetered on the brink of disintegration. As we left the restaurant and walked in
opposite directions, we could hear the child's
fading words: "Who was that, Mom? Who were
those people? Were they nice people, Mom? Do
you know those nice people, Mom . . . ?"

5

Mothers of children under three years of age are particularly in need of loving support from their husbands. It has certainly been true in our home. How well I remember the day my wife put Ryan, then four months old, on the dressing table to change his diapers. As soon as she removed the wet garments, he made like a fountain and initiated the wall and a picture of Little Boy Blue. Shirley had no sooner repaired the damage than the telephone rang; while she was gone, Ryan was struck by a sudden attack of projectile diarrhea, and he machine-gunned his crib and the rest of the nursery. By the time my patient wife had bathed her son and scoured the room, she was near exhaustion. She dressed Ryan in clean, sweet-smelling clothes and put him over her shoulder affectionately. At that moment he deposited his breakfast down her neck and into her undergarments. She told me that evening that she was going to re-read her motherhood contract to see if days like that were written in the fine print. Needless to say, the family went out to dinner that night.

No discussion of maternal fatigue would be complete without mentioning the early evening hours —unquestionably the toughest part of the day for the mother of small children. Much has been written lately about the international "energy crisis," but there is nothing on the globe to parallel the shortage of energy in a young mother between 6:00 and 9:00 P.M.! The dinner is over and the dishes are stacked. She is already tired, but now she has to get the troops in bed. She gives them their baths and pins on the diapers and brushes their teeth and puts

6

on the pajamas and reads a story and says the prayers and brings them seven glasses of water. These tasks would not be so difficult if the children *wanted* to go to bed. They most certainly do not, however, and develop extremely clever techniques for resistance and postponement. It is a pretty dumb kid who can't extend this ten-minute process into an hour-long tug of war. And when it's all finished and mom staggers through the nursery door and leans against the wall, she is then supposed to shift gears and greet her romantic lover in her own bedroom. Fat chance!

Let's look at the problem of fatigue and time pressure exclusively from the perspective of children. How do they cope with the constant rush and scurry within the family? First, children are often aware of the tension, even when we adults have learned to ignore or deny it. A father recently told me he was putting on his toddler's shoes, and he didn't even realize that he was rushing to complete the job quickly. His three-year-old quietly looked up at him and said, "Are we in a hurry again, Daddy?" Zap! The arrow struck in his heart. "Yes, son, I guess we're always in a hurry," he said with a sigh of regret.

The viewpoint of children was beautifully represented by a little nine-year-old girl, who composed her idea of what a grandmother is supposed to be. This piece was submitted by a nurse, Juanita Nelson, and appeared in the employee newspaper at Children's Hospital of Los Angeles. I think you will appreciate the incredible insight of this third grade girl.

7

What's A Grandmother?
by a third grader

A grandmother is a lady who has no children of her own. She likes other people's little girls and boys. A grandfather is a man grandmother. He goes for walks with the boys, and they talk about fishing and stuff like that.

Grandmothers don't have to do anything except to be there. They're old so they shouldn't play hard or run. It is enough if they drive us to the market where the pretend horse is, and have a lot of dimes ready. Or if they take us for walks, they should slow down past things like pretty leaves and caterpillars. They should never say "hurry-up."

Usually grandmothers are fat, but not too fat to tie your shoes. They wear glasses and funny underwear. They can take their teeth and gums off.

Grandmothers don't have to be smart, only answer questions like, "Why isn't God married?" and "How come dogs chase cats!"

Grandmothers don't talk baby talk like visitors do, because it is hard to understand. When they read to us they don't skip or mind if it is the same story over again.

Everybody should try to have a grandmother, especially if you don't have television, because they are the only grown-ups who have time.

How's that for sheer wisdom from the pen of a child? This little girl has shown us the important role played by grandparents in the lives of small children . . . especially grandparents who can take their teeth and gums off! (I am reminded of the time

8

my eleven-month-old daughter was given a hard cookie by a little boy. His older sister scolded, "She can't eat that, you dummy! She has rubber teeth!") Regardless of the condition of their molars, grandmothers and grandfathers can be invaluable to the world of little people. For one thing, "They are the only grown-ups who have time."

It is interesting that our little authoress made two references to time pressure. How badly children need adults who can go for casual walks and talk about fishing and stuff like that ... and slow down to look at pretty leaves and caterpillars ... and answer questions about God and the nature of the world as it is. I dealt with this responsibility in my book *Hide or Seek*, and feel my message should be repeated here.

Why do dedicated parents have to be reminded to be sensitive to the needs of their children, anyway? Shouldn't this be the natural expression of their love and concern? Yes, it should, but Mom and Dad have some problems of their own. They are pushed to the limits of their endurance by the pressure of time. Dad is holding down three jobs and he huffs and puffs to keep up with it all. Mom never has a free minute, either. Tomorrow night, for example, she is having eight guests for dinner and she only has this one evening to clean the house, go to the market, arrange the flowers for the centerpiece, and put the hem in the dress she will wear. Her "to do" list is three pages long and she already has a splitting headache from it all. She opens a can of "Spaghetti-os" for the kids' supper and hopes the troops will stay out of her hair. About 7 P.M., little Larry tracks down his perspiring mother and says, "Look what I just drawed, Mom." She glances downward and says, "Uh, huh," obviously thinking about something else.

Ten minutes later, Larry asks her to get him some juice. She complies but resents his intrusion. She is behind schedule and her tension is mounting. Five minutes later he interrupts again, this time wanting her to reach a toy that sits on the top shelf of the closet. She stands looking down at him for a moment and then hurries down the hall to meet his demand, mumbling as she goes. But as she passes his bedroom door, she notices that he has spread his toys all over the floor and made a mess with the glue. Mom explodes. She screams and threatens and shakes Larry till his teeth rattle.

Does this drama sound familiar? It should, for "routine panic" is becoming an American way of life. . . . There was a time when a man didn't fret if he missed a stage coach; he'd just catch it next month. Now if a fellow misses a section of a re-volving door he's thrown into despair! But guess who is the inevitable loser from this breathless life-style? It's the little guy who is leaning against the wall with his hands in the pockets of his blue jeans. He misses his father during the long day and tags around after him at night, saying, "Play ball, Dad!" But Dad is pooped. Besides, he has a briefcase full of work to be done. Mom had promised to take him to the park this afternoon but then she had to go to that Women's Auxiliary meeting at the last minute. The lad gets the message—his folks are busy again. So he drifts into the family room and watches two hours of pointless cartoons and reruns on television.

Children just don't fit into a "to do" list very well. It takes time to introduce them to good books —it takes time to listen, once more, to the skinned-knee episode and talk about the bird with the broken wing. These are the building blocks of esteem, held together with the mortar of love. But they seldom materialize amidst busy timetables. Instead, crowded lives produce fatigue—and fatigue produces irritability—and irritability produces indifference—and indifference can be interpreted by the child as a lack of genuine affection and personal esteem.

As the commercial says, "Slow down, America!" What is your rush, anyway? Don't you know your children will be gone so quickly and you will have nothing but blurred memories of those years when they needed you? I'm not suggesting that we invest our entire adult lives into the next generation, nor must everyone become parents. But once those children are here, they had better fit into our schedule somewhere. This is, however, a lonely message at the present time in our society. Others are telling Mom to go to work—have a career—do her own thing—turn her babies over to employees of the state working in child-care centers. Let someone else discipline, teach, and guide her toddler. While she's at it, though, she'd better hope that her "someone else" gets across the message of esteem and worth to that pudgy little butterball who waves "good-by" to his mommy each morning.[1]

[1]James Dobson, *Hide or Seek* (Old Tappan, N.J.: Fleming H. Revell Co., 1974), pp. 53-55. Used by permission.

Summary and Recommendations

From this discussion of the universal problem... fatigue and time pressure... what related concepts do wives most wish their husbands understood? It is my belief that feminine depression associated with the hustle and bustle of living could be reduced significantly if men comprehended and accepted the three ideas which follow:

1. For some strange reason, human beings (and particularly women) tolerate stresses and pressure much more easily if at least one other person knows they are enduring it. This principle is filed under the category of "human understanding," and it is highly relevant to housewives. The frustrations of raising small children and handling domestic duties would be much more manageable if their husbands acted like they comprehended it all. Even if a man does nothing to change the situation, simply his awareness that his wife did an admirable job today will make it easier for her to repeat the assignment tomorrow. Instead, the opposite usually occurs. At least eight million husbands will stumble into the same unforgiveable question tonight: "What did you do all day, Dear?" The very nature of the question implies that the little woman has been sitting on her rear-end watching television and drinking coffee since arising at noon! The little woman could kill him for saying it.

Everyone needs to know that he is respected for the way he meets his responsibilities. Husbands get this emotional nurture through job promotions, raises in pay, annual evaluations, and incidental praise during the work day. Women at home get it

12

from their husbands—if they get it at all. The most unhappy wives and mothers are often those who handle their fatigue and time pressure in solitude, and their men are never very sure why they always act so tired.

2. Most women will agree that the daily tasks of running a household can be managed; it is the accumulating projects that break their backs. Periodically, someone has to clean the stove and refrigerator, and replace the shelf paper, and wax the floors and clean the windows. These kinds of cyclical responsibilities are always waiting in line for the attention of a busy mother, and prevent her from ever feeling "caught up." It is my belief that *most* families can afford to hire outside help to handle these projects, and the money would be well spent for such a purpose.

The suggestion of hiring domestic help may seem highly impractical in this inflationary economy where everyone has too much "month" left at the end of the money. However, I am merely recommending that each family reevaluate how it spends its resources. This matter was first discussed in *Hide or Seek*, and at the risk of redundance, I am again quoting from that remarkable volume:

Most Americans maintain a "priority list" of things to purchase when enough money has been saved for that purpose. They plan ahead to reupholster the sofa or carpet the dining-room floor or buy a newer car. However, it is my conviction that domestic help for the mother of small children should appear on that priority list too. Without it, she is

13

sentenced to the same responsibility day in and day out, seven days a week. For several years, she is unable to escape the unending burden of dirty diapers, runny noses, and unwashed dishes. It is my belief that she will do a more efficient job in those tasks and be a better mother if she can share the load with someone else occasionally. More explicitly, I feel she should get out of the house completely for one day a week, doing something for sheer enjoyment. This seems more important to the happiness of the home than buying new drapes or a power saw for Dad.

But how can middle-class families afford housecleaning and baby-sitting services in these inflationary days? It can best be accomplished by using competent high-school students instead of older adults. I would suggest that a call be placed to the counseling office of the nearest senior high school. Tell the counselor that you need a mature, third-year student to do some cleaning. Do not reveal that you're looking for a regular employee. When the referred girl arrives, try her out for a day and see how she handles responsibility. If she's very efficient, offer her a weekly job. If she is slow and flighty, thank her for coming and call for another student that following week. There is a remarkable difference in maturity level between high-school girls, and you'll eventually find one who works like an adult.

Incidentally, if your husband is saving for that new power saw, it might be better to eliminate one of your own priority items the first time around. Either way, don't tell him I sent you.[2]

[2]Ibid., pp. 59, 60.

3. Husbands *and* wives should constantly guard against the scourge of overcommitment. Even worthwhile and enjoyable activities become damaging when they consume the last ounce of energy or the remaining free moments in the day. Though it is rarely possible for a busy family, everyone needs to waste some time every now and then—to walk along kicking rocks and thinking pleasant thoughts. Men need time to putter in the garage and women need to pluck their eyebrows and do the girlish things again. But as I have described, the whole world seems to conspire against such reconstructive activities. Even our vacations are hectic: "We have to reach St. Louis by sundown or we'll lose our reservations."

I can provide a simple prescription for a happier, healthier life, but it must be implemented by the individual family. *You* must resolve to slow your pace; you must learn to say "no" gracefully; you must resist the temptation to chase after more pleasures, more hobbies, more social entanglements; you must "hold the line" with the tenacity of a tackle for a professional football team, blocking out the intruders and defending the home team. In essence, three questions should be asked about every new activity which presents itself: Is it worthy of our time? What will be eliminated if it is added? What will be its impact on our family life? My suspicion is that most of the items in our busy day would score rather poorly on this three-item test.

You'll have to excuse me now; I'm late for an appointment. . . .

Questions and Answers

Question: How do you feel about employment for mothers of preschool children? What part does their "outside" work play in the problem of fatigue and time pressure?

Answer: It is reasonable, isn't it, that one cannot carve forty choice hours from the week for an investment in a job without imposing "fatigue and time pressure" on the remaining portion. Thus, I am strongly opposed to the mothers of *preschool* children holding down full-time employment in situations which do not require it. Yet we are currently witnessing a vast movement of women into the commercial world with numerous consequences for the home and family. As stated before, every disenchanted housewife is being offered the same solution to her low self-esteem: get a job, have a career, and do your own thing. Almost half of the women in this country are currently employed (30,370,000, according to government figures published in 1973) and the totals are rising. My viewpoint on this national trend is not likely to win many admirers within certain circles, but I can't remain silent on so important a topic. *In short, I believe that this abandonment of the home is our gravest and most dangerous mistake as a nation!*

Certainly, there are stressful financial situations which demand that a wife go to work to help support the family. And there are more serious marital disruptions where the husband either cannot work or is removed from the home for one reason or another. These problems obviously require the financial contribution of the women involved.

16

However, to sell the concept across America that every female who isn't "working" is being cheated and exploited is a lie with enormous consequences.

This falsehood is vigorously supported by two other myths which are equally foolish. The first is that *most* mothers of small children can work all day and still come home and meet their family obligations—perhaps even better than they could if they remained at home. Nonsense! There is only so much energy within the human body for expenditure during each twenty-four hours, and when it is invested in one place it is not available for use in another. It is highly improbable that the *average* woman can arise early in the morning and get her family fed and located for the day, then work from 9:00 to 5:00, drive home from 5:01 to 5:30, and still have the energy to assault her "home-work" from 5:31 until midnight. Oh, she may cook dinner and handle the major household chores, but few women alive are equipped with the superstrength necessary at the end of a workday to meet the emotional needs of their children, to train and guide and discipline, to build self-esteem, to teach the true values of life, and beyond all that, to maintain a healthy marital relationship as well. Perhaps the task can be accomplished for a week or a month, or even a season. But for years on end? I simply don't believe it. To the contrary, I have observed that exhausted wives and mothers become irritable, grouchy, and frustrated, setting the stage for conflict within the home.

Incidentally, *busy* wives must summon every ounce of creativity if they are to meet their many

17

commitments. I know one mother who had developed a unique "stalling" device for use when she is late with the preparation of dinner. She rushes into the kitchen a few minutes before her husband arrives home from work, and places one sliced onion in the heated oven. When he walks through the front door, he is greeted by a pleasant aroma of, perhaps, beef stew or enchilada pie. He is so pleased by the obvious progress in the kitchen that he settles down to read his paper and await the final product. Of course, she occasionally has to explain why tuna fish sandwiches made the house smell like onion-something-or-other.

The second myth standing on wobbly legs is that small children (those under five years of age) don't really need the extensive nurturing and involvement of their mothers, anyway. If this falsehood were accurate, it would conveniently expunge all guilt from the consciences of working women. But it simply won't square with scientific knowledge. I attended a national conference on child development held recently in Miami, Florida. Virtually every report of research presented during that three-day meeting ended with the same conclusion: the mother-child relationship is absolutely vital to healthy development of children. The final speaker of the conference, a well-known authority in this field, explained that the Russian government is currently abandoning its child-care network because they have observed the same inescapable fact: employees of the State simply cannot replace the one-to-one influence of a mother with her own child. The speaker concluded his remarks by saying

18

that feminine responsibilities are so vital to the next generation that the future of our nation actually depends on how we "see" our women. I agree.

But my intense personal opinions on this matter of "preschool mothering" are not only based on scientific evidence and professional experience. My views have also been greatly influenced within my own home. Our two children are infinitely complex, as are all children, and my wife and I want to guide the formative years ourselves. Danae is nine years old. She will be an adolescent in four more seasons, and I am admittedly jealous of anything robbing me of these remaining days of her childhood. Every moment is precious to me. Ryan is four. Not only is he in constant motion, but he is also in a state of rapid physical and emotional change. At times it is almost frightening to see how dynamic is the development of my little toddler. When I leave home for a four- or five-day speaking trip, Ryan is a noticeably different child upon my return. The building blocks for his future emotional and physical stability are clearly being laid moment by moment, stone upon stone, precept upon precept. Now I ask you who disagree with what I have written; to whom as I going to submit the task of guiding that unfolding process of development? Who will care enough to make the necessary investment if my wife and I are too busy for the job? What babysitter will take our place? What group-oriented facility can possibly provide the *individual* love and guidance which Ryan needs and deserves? Who will represent my values and beliefs to my son and daughter and be ready to answer their questions during the peak of interest? To whom will I surrender the prime-time experiences of their day? The rest of the world can make its own choice, but as for me and my house, we welcome the opportunity to shape the two little lives which have been loaned to us. And I worry about a nation which calls that task "unrewarding and unfulfilling and boring."

I know that kids can frustrate and irritate their parents, as I have described, but the rewards of raising them far outweigh the cost. Besides, nothing worth having ever comes cheap, anyway.

Question: Are you saying, then, that every woman should become a wife and mother, regardless of her other desires?

Answer: Certainly not. A woman should feel free to choose the direction her life will take. In no sense should she be urged to raise a family and abandon her own career or educational objectives, if this is not her desire. Furthermore, I regret the "old maid" image which frightens young women into marrying the first fleeting opportunity which presents itself. My strong criticism, then, is not with those who choose nonfamily life styles for themselves. Rather, it is aimed at those who abandon their parental responsibility *after* the choice has been made.

○ ○ ○

LONELINESS, ISOLATION, AND BOREDOM

Feelings of self-worth and acceptance, which provide the cornerstone of a healthy personality, can be obtained from only *one* source. It cannot be bought or manufactured. Self-esteem is only generated by what we see reflected about ourselves in the eyes of other people. It is only when others respect us that we respect ourselves. It is only when others love us that we love ourselves. It is only when others find us pleasant and desirable and worthy that we come to terms with our own egos. Occasionally, a person is created with such towering self-confidence that he doesn't seem to need the acceptance of other people, but he is indeed a rare bird. The vast majority of us are dependent on our associates for emotional sustenance each day. What does this say, then, about those who exist in a state of perpetual isolation, being deprived of loving, caring human contact year after year? Such people are virtually certain to experience feelings of worthlessness and its stepchildren, deep depression and despair.

Why do housewives, particularly, allow themselves to be sealed off from meaningful friendships and associations outside their homes? Why does their natural course seem to take them toward further loneliness and emotional deprival? I believe there are at least six explanations for the isolation of women, today, and I think we should examine each of them briefly.

1. Small children isolate a mother. It's such a hassle to pack the porta-crib and the diapers and all the supportative paraphernalia in the car, and go off to visit a friend. Mom has to wonder if it's worth the effort. Then too, the kids won't play by themselves and they keep the women from enjoying the occasion, anyway. And if the youngsters are not well disciplined, their mother is embarrassed to take them anywhere and the invitations become more scarce from her former friends who simply can't stand to have her brats in their houses. Thus, the mothers of preschool children often give up and stay at home, spending month after month predominantly in the company of "little people." I heard of one such mother who was finally given an opportunity to get out of the house. Her husband's company had prepared a banquet in honor of retiring employees, and she was seated beside the president himself. She was very nervous about talking to a real, live adult again. She feared she might revert to baby talk during the course of the evening. To her surprise, however, she conversed without a flaw through the entire meal, speaking of world events and current political conditions. Then she realized with dismay that throughout their conversation, she had been dutifully cutting the president's meat and wiping his mouth with her

napkin. I suppose you could call this a housewife's occupational hazard.

2. Though avant garde feminists may chew me to pieces for saying so, it is my observation that women can be absolutely vicious with each other. Having supervised female employees through the years, I have stood in amazement as they scratched and clawed one another over the most minor conflicts. One explosion of monumental consequence began with a disagreement among four secretaries about which deodorant was the most effective! Can you imagine four red-faced women screaming at each other over whether to spray it or roll it on?! (The "real" conflict, of course, involved resentment having nothing to do with deodorant.) I have employed two or three particularly talented antagonists who could stir up more trouble in an afternoon than I could untangle in a week. But this same competitiveness and suspicion is also represented among housewifes, I believe. There are many women who simply can't stand other women. There are other less aggressive individuals who are greatly threatened by their feminine associates. Such a woman wouldn't think of inviting "the girls" over for tea unless she had spit-shined her house inside and out, and prepared a super-delicious dessert. And those who have nicer homes will never be invited to the cottages of women who are embarrassed by their humble dwellings. And those whose husbands have professional, higher-paying jobs are often deeply resented by those who must struggle to pay the utility bills each month. In summary, women are often pitted against the very

23

people whom they need for mutual respect and acceptance. The result is loneliness and boredom.

3. Feelings of inferiority, themselves, serve to isolate women (and men) from each other. I have already stated the converse: isolation increases inferiority. These two conditions often interact in a vicious cycle, spiraling ever downward into despair and loneliness. The woman who has no friends— and I mean no "real" friends—feels too inferior to make new social contacts, and her failure to make friends makes her feel even more inferior. A housewife in this predicament is a prime candidate for "secret" alcoholism or drug abuse, or even suicide. She is desperate for meaningful contact with people, yet her behavior is often misinterpreted by her peers as being "stuck up," cold, aloof or self-sufficient.

4. Women are often less successful in finding outside interests and activities than are their masculine counterparts. Men typically love sporting events, and draw great enthusiasm from following the (televised) games of the home team. Women do not. Men usually like to hunt and fish and hike in the wilderness. Women stay home and wait for them. Men like to bowl and play golf and tennis and basketball and softball. Women watch while yawning on the sidelines. Men like to build and fix things, and work in the garage. Women remain inside washing the dishes. Men find recreation in boating and auto racing and everything mechanical. Women are bored with such nonsense. Now obviously, these are generalizations which have innumerable exceptions, but the fact remains that

men usually lack the time to pursue all their varied interests, while their wives may find it difficult to generate much genuine enthusiasm for anything. I suspect that the cultural influences of early childhood stamp a certain passivity on little girls, constricting their field of interests. For whatever reasons, the world of women is typically more narrow than that of men. For proof of this fact, listen to the conversations of the women as opposed to men at your next social gathering. The feminine discussion will probably center around children, cosmetics, and other people's behavior; the men will talk about a much greater variety of topics. It should not be surprising then, that boredom ranks high as a source of depression among women.

5. Fatigue and time pressure, discussed earlier, must also serve to isolate the mothers of small children. There simply isn't enough time and energy to open the door to the outside world.

6. Financial limitations in an inflationary economy certainly restrict the activities of housewives.

Certainly, there are many reasons why housewives can find themselves lonely, isolated, and bored, even if they live in the midst of six million other lonely people. And what agitation is caused by their emptiness. One writer said, "Everybody must be somebody to somebody to be anybody!" I agree. A lyricist expressed a similar concept in his song entitled, "You're Nobody till Somebody Loves You." Dr. William Glasser explained this same psychological principle in his popular text *Reality Therapy*: "At all times in our lives we must have at least one person who cares about us and whom we care for ourselves. If we do not have this essential person, we will not be able to fulfill our basic needs." Obviously, we human beings are social animals and must continually depend on each other for emotional stability.

Emotional Differences Between Men and Women

At this point I offer a message of great importance to every husband who loves and wants to understand his wife. Whereas men and women have the same needs for self-worth and belonging, they typically satisfy those needs differently. A man derives his sense of worth primarily from the reputation he earns in his job or profession. He draws emotional satisfaction from achieving in business, becoming financially independent, developing a highly respected craft or skill, supervising others, becoming "boss," or by being loved and appreciated by his patients or clients or fellow businessmen. The man who is successful in these areas does not depend on his wife as his *primary* shield against inferiority. Of course, she plays an important role as his companion and lover, but she isn't essential to his self-respect day by day.

By contrast, a housewife approaches her marriage from a totally different perspective. She does not have access to "other" sources of self-esteem commonly available to her husband. She can cook a good dinner, but once it is eaten her family may not even remember to thank her for it. Her household duties do not bring her respect in the community, and she is not likely to be praised for the quality of her dusting techniques. Therefore, the more isolated she becomes, the more vital her man will be to her sense of fulfillment, confidence, and well-being. He must be that "one person" of whom Dr. Glasser wrote, and if he is not, she is "unable to fulfill her basic needs." That spells trouble with a capital T.

Let's reduce it to a useful oversimplification: men derive self-esteem by being *respected*; women feel worthy when they are *loved*. This may be the most important personality distinction between the sexes.

This understanding helps explain the unique views of marriage as seen by men and women. A man can be contented with a kind of business partnership in marriage, provided sexual privileges are part of the arrangement. As long as his wife prepares his dinner each evening, is reasonably amiable, and doesn't nag him during football season, he can be satisfied. The romantic element is nice—but not necessary. However, this kind of surface relationship drives his wife utterly wild with frustration. She must have something more meaningful. Women yearn to be the special sweethearts of their men, being respected and appreciated and loved with tenderness. This is why a housewife often thinks about her husband during the day and eagerly awaits his arrival home; it explains why their wedding anniversary is more important to her, and why he gets clobbered when he forgets it. It explains why she is constantly "reaching" for him when he is at home, trying to pull him out of

27

the newspaper or television set; it explains why *Absence of Romantic Love in My Marriage* ranked so high in my poll as a source of depression among women, whereas men would have rated it somewhere in the vicinity of last place.

Women often find it impossible to convey their needs for romantic affection to their husbands. One fellow listened carefully as I explained the frustration his wife had expressed to me; he promptly went out and bought some flowers for her and rang the front doorbell. When she opened the door, he extended his arm and said, "Here!" Having met his marital responsibilities, he pushed past her and turned on the television set. His wife was not exactly overwhelmed by his generosity.

Another man said, "I just don't understand my wife. She has everything she could possibly want. She has a dishwasher and a new dryer, and we live in a nice neighborhood. I don't drink or beat the kids or kick the dog. I've been faithful since the day we were married. But she's miserable and I can't figure out why!" His love-starved wife would have traded the dishwasher, the dryer, and the dog for a single expression of genuine tenderness from her unromantic husband. Appliances do not build self-esteem; being somebody's sweetheart most certainly does.

Instead of building confidence and preserving romantic excitement, many men seem determined to do the opposite, particularly in public. Have you ever watched a person (usually a man) play the popular game called "Assassinate the Spouse?" Any number of couples can play this destructive game, and its objective is simple: each contestant attempts to punish his mate by ridiculing and embarrassing her in front of their friends. Although he can hurt her verbally when they are alone, he can cut her to pieces when onlookers are present. And if he wants to be especially vicious, he lets the guests know he thinks she is dumb and ugly; those are the two places where she is most vulnerable. Bonus points are awarded if he can reduce her to tears.

Why would anyone want to publicize his (or her) resentment in this manner? The reason is that hostility seeks its own ventilation, and most angry people find their feelings difficult to contain. But how unfortunate is the couple who slug it out before spectators. This brutal game has no winners; the contest ends when one player is totally divested of his self-respect and dignity.

I have often wished there were an acceptable method for men and women to ventilate their feelings in private. A golfer can pound the ball around an eighteen-hole course, and somehow feel more tranquil in the clubhouse. Weekend basketball players throw their elbows at each other in the gymnasium and thereby reduce their frustrations and tensions. Professional hockey players unload their anxieties by smashing their opponents with their sticks and skates. Unfortunately, however, there is no convenient method for husbands and wives to work out their hostilities. They can only glare at each other in silence across a room. I have given considerable thought to this problem and believe I have a workable solution. I am proposing that every well-designed home of the future be equipped with a bumper car rink—the kind that is found at all state fairgrounds and amusement parks. If you've ever watched the drivers of these vehicles smashing each other at full speed, you've seen their dilated eyes and the wicked grins on their faces. They bellow with delight when they catch an unsuspecting driver broadside, knocking his car across the rink. Wouldn't it be great if a husband and wife could schedule one hour a day, probably from 5 to 6 P.M., on a bumper car track? I can hear them muttering as they smash each others' cars: "Hah! That's what you get for being so stingy with our money!" or "Take that!" (Wham!) "That'll teach you to be so grouchy when you come home." After fifty hits each, a bell would ring, signaling the end of the hour, and the two "cleansed" drivers would emerge as lovely friends for the remainder of the evening. Do you suppose the world is ready for this remedy just yet?

The 5000-Year-Old Solution

There is still no substitute for the biblical prescription for marriage, nor will its wisdom ever be replaced. A successful husband and wife relationship begins with the attitude of the man; he has been ordained by God as the head of the family, and the responsibility for its welfare rests upon his shoulders. This charge can be found in the early writings of Moses in the Old Testament, returning at least 5000 years into Jewish history. Deuteronomy 24:5 (TLB) reads:

A newly married man is not to be drafted into the army nor given any other responsibilities; for a year he shall be free to be at home, happy with his wife.

Imagine the luxury! Newlyweds were given one full year in which to adjust to married life, with no responsibilities or duties during that period. (I must admit that I don't know what they did with their time after the first three weeks, but it sounds like fun, anyway.) Compare it with the first year of marriage in this day, when the man and woman are both working, going to school, and all too frequently the bride is facing the biological, emotional, and financial tensions of a pregnancy. But my point in quoting this Scripture is better illustrated by the last sentence as stated in the King James Version. It reads, "And he (the husband) shall *cheer up* his wife which he hath taken."

Early Mosaic law made it clear that the emotional well-being of a wife is the specific responsibility of her husband. It was his job to "cheer" her. Friends and neighbors, it still is! This message is for the man whose own ego needs have drawn him to achieve super success in life, working seven days a week and consuming himself in a continual quest for power and status. If his wife and children do not fit into his schedule somewhere, he deserves the conflict that is certainly coming. This masculine charge should also be heeded by the husband who hoards his nonworking hours for his own pleasures, fishing every weekend, burying his head in the television set, or living on a golf course. Everyone needs recreation and these activities have an important reconstructive role to play. But when our enjoyment begins to suffocate those who need us—those whose very existence depends on our commitment—it has gone too far and requires regulation.

Derek Prince has expressed this viewpoint even more strongly. He feels that the troubles America is facing, particularly with reference to the family, can be traced to what he calls "renegade males." The word renegade actually means "one who has reneged." We men have ignored our God-given responsibility to care for the welfare of our families, to discipline our children, to supervise the expenditure of the financial resources, to assume spiritual leadership, to love and to cherish and protect. Instead, we have launched ourselves on a lifetime ego trip, thinking only of our needs and our pleasures and our status. Is it any wonder that low self-esteem is a problem among our women? Is it surprising that loneliness, isolation, and boredom have reached critical proportions? Both these canyons of depression are dug by the deterioration of relationships between husbands and wives, and we men are in the best position to improve the situation.

Am I recommending that men dominate their wives, ruling with an iron fist and robbing them of individuality? Certainly not. Again, the prescription for a successful marriage is found in the Bible, where the concept of the family originated. God, who created the entire universe, should be able to tell us how to live together harmoniously. He has done just that, as written in Ephesians 5:28-33 (TLB).

32

That is how husbands should treat their wives, loving them as part of themselves. For since a man and his wife are now one, a man is really doing himself a favor and loving himself when he loves his wife! No one hates his own body but lovingly cares for it, just as Christ cares for his body the Church, of which we are parts. (That the husband and wife are one body is proved by the Scripture which says, "A man must leave his father and mother when he marries, so that he can be perfectly joined to his wife, and the two shall be one!") I know this is hard to understand, but it is an illustration of the way we are parts of the body of Christ. So again I say, a man must love his wife as a part of himself; and the wife must see to it that she deeply respects her husband, obeying, praising, and honoring him.

There is certainly no room for masculine oppression within that formula. The husband is charged with loving leadership within the family, but he must recognize his wife's feelings and needs as being one with his own. When she hurts, he hurts, and takes steps to end the pain. What she wants, he wants, and satisfies her needs. And through all this, his wife deeply respects, praises and even obeys her loving husband. If this one prescription were applied within the American family, we would have little need for divorce courts, alimony, visiting rights, crushed children, broken hearts, and shattered lives.

Now, if we appear to be blaming all marital and family woes on husbands, let me clarify the point. For every complaint women have against men, there is a corresponding bellyache on the other end of the line. And I'm certain that I've heard them all. Women can be just as selfish and irresponsible as their men. How many wives have "let themselves go," waddling around on massive rhino haunches and looking like they had spent the night in a tornado? How many husbands come home every night to a wrecked house, dirty kids, and a nagging, groaning, overindulged wife? King Solomon must have known such a sweetheart, for he wrote:

It is better to live in the corner of an attic than with a crabby woman in a lovely home (Proverbs 21:9, TLB).

Neither sex has a monopoly on offensive behavior.

But for those who accept God's design for the family, it is clear that husbands bear the *initial* responsibility for correcting the problem. This obligation is implicit in the role of leadership assigned to males. Where does it begin? By men treating their wives with the same dignity and attention that they give to their own bodies, "loving them even as Christ loved the Church, giving his life for it." What a challenge! If this be male chauvinism, then may the whole masculine world be swept by its philosophy.

Would it be ostentatious for me to give a personal illustration at this point? I hope not, and ask that the reader not interpret this statement as boasting. My wife, Shirley, and I have applied the biblical prescription in our own marriage, and have found it valid and true. Having been with Shirley daily

34

since we were married fourteen years ago, I still enjoy the pleasure of her company. In fact, if I could choose anyone on earth with whom to spend a free evening, Shirley would rank at the top of the list. She feels the same way about me, which is even more remarkable! I suppose it can be summarized this way: Shirley and I are not just married to one another; we are also "best friends." Does this mean that we never have strong differences of opinion? Certainly not. Does it mean that we float along on a pink cloud of adolescent romanticism every day of our lives? No chance. Does it mean that irritability and other human frailties have been conquered? Not likely. Perhaps I should tell you about our one absolutely unresolvable problem; there is an area of difficulty between us which defies correction or mediation, and I have even lost hope of ever coming to terms with it: Shirley and I operate on totally different thermostats. Even though we have become "one body" we have vastly differing ideas of how hot it should be! My wife is cold at least eleven months out of the year, thawing momentarily during the summer. She warmed up last August 14 for about an hour, right around noon, and then froze over again. Wouldn't you know that I stay overheated the year around, and gasp for a cool breeze in the California sunshine. This differing viewpoint produces some dramatic struggles for control of the heating unit in our home. A man's home is his castle they say, but in my case, it's a furnace.

Obviously, the success of my relationship with Shirley does not result from human perfection on either part. It is simply a product of caring for the feelings, needs, and concerns of the other. It is giving, not grabbing. Or as it is stated in the marriage vows, "In honor, preferring one another." And by some strange quirk of human nature, that attitude produces self-esteem by the bushel.

A Closer Look at Reality

We cannot ignore the plight of the woman whose husband "ought to" but doesn't. What should be her attitude if he is continually unsympathetic to her emotional needs and longings? What if he refuses to accept his designated role as the loving, caring leader of the family? How should a wife cope with emotional abandonment, playing second fiddle to his job, or televised sports, or a consuming hobby, or even another woman? It would be almost unethical for me to write on the subject of depression in women without confronting these issues head-on, for if my observations are accurate, *most* women have sought to answer those lingering questions for themselves.

Before offering my views on this subject, however, let's pause to examine the suggestions of others. Let's suppose that a lonely, discouraged wife visits her local bookstore to seek advice and counsel in the writings of the "experts." Assuming that the most popular books would probably provide the greatest help, she examines the more prominently displayed volumes in the marriage and family section of the store. The first text that she considers is entitled *Open Marriage*, which proclaims itself to

36

be the Number One Bestseller in America. If she buys and reads it, she will learn that marriage is far healthier when swinging husbands and wives keep a little hanky-panky going on the side. Get the message, now! A man and woman, so the authors say, will be inexorably drawn together by knowing that their mate may be sleeping with someone new tomorrow night.

Sitting beside *Open Marriage* on the top shelf is another bestseller which would tell our depressed friend to sabotage her marriage altogether. It is entitled *Creative Divorce*, and proposes some innovative concepts, among them, "Divorce is not the end . . . it is the beginning. Make it work for you," and "To say goodbye is to say hello. Hello to a new life . . . to a new freer, more self-assured you. Hello to new ways of looking at the world and of relating to people. Your divorce can be the very best thing that ever happened to you!" How's that for an original approach to family life? Kick the bum out of the house and giggle your way into a world of continual delight and bliss. If our housewife is given this irresponsible suggestion at the precise moment of her greatest despair, she may turn her sick marriage into a dead one. Every physician knows that it is easy to kill his patient; the skill comes in curing him. Yet in *Creative Divorce*, the "patient" is told to ignore all other medications and remedies that might restore the health and vitality of his family life. I wish I knew how many marriages this single book has destroyed.

Obviously, the irresponsible, destructive "solutions" to knotty problems are not difficult to generate. They have always been easier to develop than those which provide a way out of the mire. Admittedly, I don't possess every answer to the problems I have posed. I know of no magical tricks that will turn a cold, unresponsive man into a compassionate, communicative, romantic dream machine. But I can offer some suggestions which I have found to be helpful in my counseling experience.

First, a woman who wants to reignite the romantic fires in her husband must look for ways to *teach* him about her needs. Men have different emotional needs than women, making it hard for them to comprehend the feelings and longings of their wives. To correct this lack of understanding, women often resort to nagging, pleading, scolding, complaining and accusing. This is how it sounds to an exhausted man who has come home from work moments before: "Won't you just put down that newspaper, George, and give me five minutes of your time? Five minutes—is that too much to ask? You never seem to care about my feelings, anyway. How long has it been since we went out for dinner? Even if we did, you'd probably take the newspaper along with you. I'll tell you, George, sometimes I think you don't care about me and the kids anymore. If just once ... just once ... you would show a little love and understanding, I would drop dead from sheer shock, etc., etc., etc."

I hope my feminine readers know that this verbal barrage at the end of a work day is *not* what I mean by teaching. It's like pounding George behind the ear with a two-by-four, and it rarely achieves more than a snarl when he gets up from the floor. Nagging shuts down communication with amazing efficiency. By contrast, teaching is a matter of timing, setting and manner.

1. *Timing.* Select the moment when your husband is typically more responsive and pleasant; perhaps that opportunity will occur immediately after the evening meal, or when the light goes out at night, or in the freshness of the morning. The worst time of the day is during the first sixty minutes after he arrives home from work, yet this is the usual combat hour. Don't lumber into such a heavy debate without giving it proper planning and forethought, taking advantage of every opportunity for the success of the effort.

2. *Setting.* The ideal situation is to ask your husband to take you on an overnight or weekend trip to a pleasant area. If financial considerations will cause him to decline, save the money out of household funds or other resources. If it is impossible to get away, the next best alternative is to obtain a babysitter and go out to breakfast or dinner alone. If that too is out of the question, then select a time at home when the children are occupied and the phone can be taken off the hook. Generally speaking, however, the farther you can get him from home, with its cares and problems and stresses, the better will be your chance to achieve genuine communication.

3. *Manner.* It is extremely important that your husband does not view your conversation as a per-

sonal attack. We are all equipped with emotional defenses which rise to our aid when we are being vilified. Don't trigger those defensive mechanisms. Instead, your manner should be as warm, loving, and supportive as possible under the circumstances. Let it be known that you are attempting to interpret *your* needs and desires, not *his* inadequacies and shortcomings. Furthermore, you must take his emotional state into consideration, as well. Postpone the conversation if he is under unusual stress from his work, or if he isn't feeling well, or if he has recently been stung by circumstances and events. Then when the timing, setting, and manner converge to produce a moment of opportunity, express your deep feelings as effectively as possible. Use the earlier sections of this book for ammunition, and like every good boy scout: be *prepared*.

Of course, one conversation is rarely sufficient to produce a long-term change in behavior and attitude. The woman who wants to be understood will continually teach her husband about her feelings and desires, while doing her best to meet his unique needs.

Am I suggesting that a woman should crawl on her belly like a subservient puppy, begging her master for a pat on the head? Certainly not! It is of the highest priority to maintain a distinct element of dignity and self-respect *throughout* the husband-wife relationship. This takes us into a related area that requires the greatest emphasis. I have observed that many (if not most) marriages suffer from a failure to recognize a universal characteristic of human nature. *We value that which we are fortunate to get; we discredit that with which we are stuck! We lust for the very thing which is beyond our grasp; we disdain that same item when it becomes a permanent possession.* No toy is ever as much fun to play with as it appeared to a wide-eyed child in a store. Seldom does an expensive automobile provide the satisfaction anticipated by the man who dreamed of its ownership. This principle is even more dramatically accurate in romantic affairs, particularly with reference to men. Let's look at the extreme case of a Don Juan, the perpetual lover who romps from one feminine flower to another. His heart throbs and pants after the elusive princess who drops her glass slipper as she flees. Every ounce of energy is focused on her capture. However, the intensity of his desire is dependent on her unavailability. The moment his passionate dreams materialize, he begins to ask himself, "Is this what I really want?" Farther down the line as the relationship progresses toward the routine circumstances of everyday life, he is attracted by new princesses and begins to wonder how he can escape the older model.

Forgive the redundancy, but I must restate the principle: *we crave that which we can't attain, but we disrespect that which we can't escape.* This axiom is particularly relevant in romantic matters, and has probably influenced *your* love life, too. Now, the forgotten part of this characteristic is that marriage does not erase or change it. Whenever one marriage partner grovels in his own disrespect . . . when he reveals his fear of rejection by his mate . . . when he begs and pleads for a handout . . . he often

41

faces a bewildering attitude of disdain from the one he needs and loves. Just as in the premarital relationship, nothing douses more water on a romantic flame than for one partner to fling himself emotionally on the other, accepting disrespect in stride. He says in effect, "No matter how badly you treat me, I'll still be here at your feet, because I can't survive without you." That is the best way I know to kill a beautiful friendship.

So what am I recommending . . . that husbands and wives scratch and claw each other to show their independence? No! That they play a sneaky cat and mouse game to recreate a "challenge"? Not at all! I am merely suggesting that self-respect and dignity be maintained in the relationship. Let's look at a case in point.

Suppose that one partner, the husband, begins to show signs of disinterest in his wife. Let's say that their sex life has been rather dull lately, and the sense of emotional togetherness is more of a memory than a reality. (The decline of a marriage is rarely brought about by a blowout; it's usually a slow leak.) Then the relationship reaches a low point and the husband consistently treats his wife rudely and disrespectfully in public, pulling behind a wall of silence when they are at home. These are symptoms of a condition which I call "the trapped syndrome." More often than not, the man is thinking these kinds of thoughts: "I'm 35 years old" (or whatever age) "and I'm not getting any younger. Do I really want to spend the rest of my life with this one woman? I'm bored with her and there are others who interest me more. But there's no way out 'cause I'm stuck." These are the feelings which usually precede esoteric infidelity, and they certainly can be felt in the strain between a husband and wife.

How should a woman respond when she reads the cues and realizes that her husband feels trapped? Obviously, the worst thing she could do is reinforce the cage around him, yet that is likely to be her initial reaction. As she thinks about how important he is to her, and what-on-earth she would do without him, and whether he's involved with another woman, her anxiety may compel her to grab and hold him. Her begging and pleading only drive him to disrespect her more, and the relationship continues to splinter. There is a better way which I have found productive in counseling experience. The most successful approach to bringing a partner back toward the center of a relationship is not to follow when he moves away from it. Instead of saying, "Why do you do me this way?" and "Why won't you talk to me?" and "Why don't you care anymore?" a wife should pull back a few inches herself. When she passes her husband in the hall and would ordinarily touch him or seek his attention, she should move by him without notice. Silence by him is greeted by silence in return. She should not be hostile or aggressive, ready to explode when he finally asks her to say what is on her mind. Rather, she responds in kind . . . being quietly confident, independent and mysterious. The effect of this behavior is to open the door on his trap. Instead of clamping herself to his neck like a blood-sucking leech, she releases her grip and introduces a certain

43

challenge in his mind, as well. He may begin to wonder if he has gone too far and may be losing something precious to him. If that will not turn him around, then the relationship is stone, cold dead.

I haven't suggested that women rise up in anger —that they stamp their feet and demand their domestic rights, or that they sulk and pout in silence. Please do not associate me with those contemporary voices which are mobilizing feminine troops for all-out sexual combat. Nothing is less attractive to me than an angry woman who is determined to grab her share, one way or the other. No, the answer is not found in hostile aggression, but in quiet self-respect!

In short, personal dignity in a marriage is maintained the same way it was produced during the dating days. The attitude should be, "I love you and am totally committed to you, but I only control my half of the relationship. I can't demand your love in return. You came to me of your free will when we agreed to marry. No one forced us together. That same free will is necessary to keep our love alive. If you choose to walk away from me, I will be crushed and hurt beyond description, because I have withheld nothing of myself. Nevertheless, I will let you go and ultimately I will survive. I couldn't demand your affection in the beginning, and I can only request it now."

Returning to the recommendation that a woman "teach" her husband about her needs, it can be done within the atmosphere of self-respect that I have described. In fact, it *must* be handled in that manner.

The Meaning of Love

It has been of concern to me that many young people grow up with a very distorted concept of romantic love. They are taught to confuse the real thing with infatuation and to idealize marriage into something it can never be. To help remedy this situation, I developed a brief true or false test for use in teaching groups of teen-agers. But to my surprise, I found that adults do not score much higher on the quiz than their adolescent offspring.

While there are undoubtedly some differences of opinion regarding the answers for this quiz, I feel strongly about what I consider to be correct responses to each item. In fact, I believe many of the common marital hang-ups develop from a misunderstanding of these ten issues. The confusion begins when boy meets girl and the entire sky lights up in romantic profusion. Smoke and fire are followed by lightning and thunder, and alas, two trembly-voiced adolescents find themselves knee deep in true love. Adrenalin and sixty-four other hormones are dumped into the cardio-vascular system by the pint, and every nerve is charged with 110 volts of electricity. Then two little fellows go racing up the respective backbones and blast their exhilarating message into each spinning head: "This is it! The search is over! You've found the perfect human being! Hooray for love!"

For our romantic young couple, it is simply too wonderful to behold. They want to be together twenty-four hours a day... to take walks in the rain and sit by the fire and kiss and munch and cuddle. They get all choked up just thinking about each other. And it doesn't take long for the subject of marriage to arise. So they set the date and reserve the chapel and contact the minister and order the flowers. The big night arrives, amidst mother's tears and dad's grins and jealous bridesmaids and bratty little flower-girls. The candles are lit and two beautiful songs are butchered by the bride's sister. Then the vows are muttered and the rings are placed on trembling fingers, and the preacher tells the groom to kiss his new wife. Then they sprint up the aisle, each flashing thirty-two teeth, on the way to the reception room. Their friends and well-wishers hug and kiss the bride and roll their eyes at the groom, and eat the awful cake and follow the instructions of the perspiring photographer. Finally, the new Mr. and Mrs. run from the church in a flurry of rice and confetti and strike out on their honeymoon. So far the beautiful dream remains intact, but it is living on borrowed time.

The first night in the motel is not only less exciting than advertised . . . it turns into a comical disaster. She is exhausted and tense and he is self-conscious and phony. From the beginning, sex is tinged with the threat of possible failure. Their vast expectations about the marital bed lead to disappointment and frustration and fear. Since most human beings have a neurotic desire to feel sexually adequate, each partner tends to blame his mate for their orgasmic problems, which will eventually add a note of anger and resentment to their relationship.

About three o'clock on the second afternoon, he

46

gives ten minutes serious thought to the fateful question, "Have I made an enormous mistake?" His silence increases her anxieties, and the seeds of disenchantment are born. Each partner has far too much time to think about the consequences of this new relationship, and they both begin to feel trapped.

Their initial argument is a silly thing; they struggle momentarily over how much money to spend for dinner on the third night of the honeymoon. She wants to go someplace romantic to charge up the atmosphere, and he wants to eat with Ronald McDonald. The flare-up only lasts a few moments and is followed by apologies, but some harsh words have been exchanged which took the keen edge off the beautiful dream. They will soon learn to hurt each other more effectively.

Somehow, they make it through the six-day trip and drive home to set up house together. Then the world starts to splinter and disentegrate before their eyes. The next fight is bigger and better than the first; he leaves home for two hours and she calls her mother. Throughout the first year, they will be engaged in an enormous contest of wills, each vying for power and leadership. And in the midst of this tug of war, she staggers out of the obstetrician's office with the words ringing in her ears, "I have some good news for you, Mrs. Jones!" If there is anything on earth Mrs. Jones doesn't need at that time, it is "good news" from an obstetrician.

From there to the final conflict, we see two disappointed, confused and deeply hurt young people, wondering how it all came about. We also see a

47

little tow-headed lad who will never enjoy the benefits of a stable home. He'll be raised by his mother and will always wonder, "Why doesn't Dad live here anymore?"

The picture I have painted does not reflect every young marriage, obviously, but it accurately represents far too many of them. The divorce rate is higher in America than in any other civilized nation in the world, and it is rising. In the case of our disillusioned young couple, what happened to their romantic dream? How did the relationship that began with such enthusiasm turn so quickly into hatred and hostility? They could not possibly have been more enamored with each other at the beginning, but their "happiness" blew up in their startled faces. Why didn't it last? How can others avoid the same unpleasant surprise?

We need to understand the true meaning of romantic love. Perhaps the answers to our quiz will help accomplish that objective.

1. *I believe love at first sight occurs between some people.* Though some readers will disagree with me, love at first sight is a physical and emotional impossibility. Why? Because love is not simply a feeling of romantic excitement; it is more than a desire to marry a potential partner; it goes beyond intense sexual attraction; it exceeds the thrill at having "captured" a highly desirable social prize. These are emotions that are unleashed at first sight, but they *do not constitute love*. I wish the whole world knew that fact. These temporary feelings differ from love in that they place the spotlight on the one experi-

encing them. "What is happening to *me*?! This is the most fantastic thing *I've* ever been through! *I* think *I* am in love!" You see, these emotions are selfish in the sense that they are motivated by our gratification. They have little to do with the new lover. Such a person has not fallen in love with another person; *he has fallen in love with love!* And there is an enormous difference between the two.

Real love, in contrast to popular notions, is an expression of the deepest appreciation for another human being; it is an intense awareness of his or her needs and longings—past, present, and future. It is unselfish and giving and caring. And believe me, friends, these are not attitudes one "falls" into at first sight, as though we were tumbling into a ditch. I have developed a lifelong love for my wife, but it was not something I fell into. I *grew* into it, and that process took time. I had to know her before I could appreciate the depth and stability of her character —to become acquainted with the nuances of her personality, which I now cherish. The familiarity from which love has blossomed simply could not be generated on "Some enchanted evening, across a crowded room." One canot love an unknown object, regardless of how attractive or sexy or nubile it is!

2. *I believe it is easy to distinguish real love from infatuation.* The answer is, again, false. That wild ride at the start of a romantic adventure bears all the earmarks of a lifetime trip. Just try to tell a starry-eyed sixteen-year-old dreamer that he is not really in love . . . that he's merely infatuated. He'll

whip out his guitar and sing you a song. "Young luv, true luv, filled with real emo-shun. Young luv, true luv, filled with true devo-shun!" He knows what he feels, and he feels great. But he'd better enjoy the roller coaster ride while it lasts, because it has a predictable end point.

I must stress this fact with the greatest emphasis: The exhilaration of infatuation is *never* a permanent condition. Period! If you expect to live on the top of that mountain, year after year, you can forget it! Emotions swing from high to low to high in cyclical rhythm, and since romantic excitement is an emotion, it too will certainly oscillate. Therefore, if the thrill of sexual encounter is identified as geuine love, then disillusionment and disappointment are already knocking at the door.

How many vulnerable young couples "fall in love" with love on the first date . . . and lock themselves in marriage before the natural swing of their emotions has even progressed through the first dip? They then wake up one morning without that neat feeling and conclude that love has died. In reality, it was never there in the first place. They were fooled by an emotional "high."

Even when a man and woman love each other deeply and genuinely, they will find themselves supercharged on one occasion and emotionally bland on another! *However, their love is not defined by the highs and lows, but is dependent on a commitment of their will!*

How can real love be distinguished from temporary infatuation? If the feeling is unreliable, how can one assess the commitment of his will? There is only one answer to that question: It takes time. The best advice I can give a couple contemplating marriage (or any other important decision) is this: make *no* important, life-shaping decisions quickly or impulsively, and when in doubt, stall for time.

3. *I believe people who sincerely love each other will not fight and argue.* I doubt if this third item actually requires an answer. Some marital conflict is as inevitable as the sunrise, even in loving marriages. There is a difference, however, between healthy and unhealthy combat, depending on the way the disagreement is handled. In an unstable marriage, the hostility is usually hurled directly at the partner: "You never do anything right; why did I ever marry you? You are incredibly dumb and you're getting more like your mother every day." These personal comments strike at the heart of one's self-worth and produce an internal upheaval. They often cause the wounded partner to respond in like manner, hurling back every unkind and hateful remark he can concoct, punctuated with tears and profanity. The avowed purpose of this kind of in-fighting is to hurt, and the words will never be forgotten, even though uttered in a moment of irrational anger. Obviously, such vicious combat is extremely damaging to a marital relationship. Healthy conflict, on the other hand, remains focused on the issue around which the disagreement began: "You are spending money faster than I can earn it!" "It upsets me when you don't tell me you'll be late for dinner." "I was embarrassed when you made me look foolish at the party last night." These areas of struggle, though

admittedly emotional and tense, are much less damaging to the egos of the opposing forces. A healthy couple can work through them by compromise and negotiation with few imbedded barbs to pluck out the following morning.

The ability to fight *properly* may be the most important concept to be learned by newlyweds. Those who never comprehend the technique are usually left with two alternatives: (1) turn the anger and resentment inward in silence, where it will fester and accumulate through the years, or (2) blast away at the personhood of one's mate. The divorce courts are well represented by couples in both categories.

4. *I believe God selects one particular person for each of us to marry, and he will guide us together.* Anyone who believes that God guarantees a successful marriage to every Christian is in for a shock. This is not to say that he is disinterested in the choice of a mate, or that he will not answer a specific request for guidance on this all-important decision. Certainly, his will should be sought in such a critical matter, and I consulted him repeatedly before proposing to my wife. However, I do not believe that God performs a routine match-making service for everyone who worships him. He has given us judgment, common sense, and discretionary powers, and he expects us to exercise these abilities in matters matrimonial. Those who believe otherwise are likely to enter marriage glibly, thinking, "God would have blocked this development if he didn't

approve of it." To such confident people I can only say, "Lotsa luck."

5. *I believe if a man and woman genuinely love each other, then hardships and troubles will have little or no effect on their relationship.* Another common misconception about the meaning of "true love" is that it inevitably stands like the rock of Gibraltar against the storms of life. Many people apparently believe that love is destined to conquer all; the Beatles endorsed this notion with their song, "All we need is love, love, love is all we need." Unfortunately, we need a bit more.

The fiber of love can be weakened by financial hardships, disease, business setbacks, or prolonged separation. Love is vulnerable to pain and trauma, and often wobbles when assaulted by life.

6. *I believe it is better to marry the wrong person than to remain single and lonely throughout life.* Again, the answer is false. Generally speaking, it is less painful to be searching for an end to loneliness than to be embroiled in the emotional combat of a sour marriage. Yet the threat of being an "old maid" (a term I detest) causes many girls to grab the first train that rambles down the marital track. And too often, it offers a one-way ticket to disaster.

7. *I believe it is not harmful to have sexual intercourse before marriage, if the couple has a meaningful relationship.* This item represents *the* most dangerous of the popular misconceptions about romantic love,

53

both for individuals and for our future as a nation. During the past fifteen years we have witnessed the tragic disintegration of our sexual mores and traditional concepts of morality. Responding to a steady onslaught by the entertainment industry and by the media, our people have begun to believe that premarital intercourse is a noble experience, and extramarital encounters are healthy, and homosexuality is acceptable, and bisexuality is even better. These views reflect the sexual stupidity of the age in which we live, yet they are believed and applied by millions of American citizens. A recent study of college students revealed that 25 percent of them have shared bedrooms with a member of the opposite sex for at least three months. According to *Life Styles and Campus Communities*, 66 percent of college students reportedly believe premarital intercourse is acceptable between any two people who consent or "when a couple has dated some and care a lot about each other." I have never considered myself to be a prophet of doom, but I am admittedly alarmed by statistical evidence of this nature. I view these trends with fear and trepidation, seeing in them the potential death of our society and our way of life.

Mankind has known intuitively for at least fifty centuries that indiscriminate sexual activity represented both an individual and a corporate threat to survival. The wisdom of those years has now been documented. Anthropologist J. D. Unwin conducted an exhaustive study of the eight-eight civilizations which have existed in the history of the world. Each culture has reflected a similar life

54

cycle, beginning with a strict code of sexual conduct and ending with the demand for complete "freedom" to express individual passion. Unwin reports that *every* society which extended sexual permissiveness to its people was soon to perish. There have been no exceptions.

Why do you suppose the reproductive urge within us is so relevant to cultural survival? It is because the energy which holds a people together is sexual in nature! The physical attraction between men and women causes them to establish a family and invest themselves in its development. It is this force which encourages them to work and save and toil to insure the survival of their families. This sexual energy provides the impetus for the raising of healthy children and for the transfer of values from one generation to the next. It urges a man to work when he would rather play. It causes a woman to save when she would rather spend. In short, the sexual aspect of our nature—when released exclusively within the family—produces stability and responsibility that would not otherwise occur. And when a nation is composed of millions of devoted, responsible family units, the entire society is stable and responsible and resilient.

If sexual energy within the family is the key to a healthy society, then its release outside those boundaries is potentially catastrophic. The very force which binds a people together then becomes the agent for its own destruction.

Who can deny that a society is seriously weakened when the intense sexual urge between men and women becomes an instrument for suspicion and intrigue within millions of individual families . . . when a woman never knows what her husband is doing when away from home . . . when a husband can't trust his wife in his absence . . . when half of the brides are pregnant at the altar . . . when each newlywed has slept with numerous partners, losing the exclusive wonder of the marital bed . . . when everyone is doing his own thing, particularly that which brings him immediate sensual gratification! Unfortunately, the most devastated victim of an immoral society of this nature is the vulnerable little child who hears his parents scream and argue; their tension and frustrations spill over into his world, and the instability of his home leaves its ugly scars on his young mind. Then he watches his parents separate in anger, and he says, "goodbye" to the father he needs and loves. Or perhaps we should speak of the thousands of babies born to un-married teen-age mothers each year, many of whom will never know the meaning of a warm, nurturing home. Or maybe we should discuss the rampant scourge of venereal disease which has reached epidemic proportions among America's youth. This is the true vomitus of the sexual revolution, and I am tired of hearing it romanticized and glorified. God has clearly forbidden irresponsible sexual behavior, not to deprive us of fun and pleasure, but to spare us the disastrous consequences of this festering way of life. Those individuals, and those nations, which choose to defy his commandments on this issue will pay a dear price for their folly. My views on this subject may be unpopular, but I believe them with everything within me!

8. *I believe if a couple is genuinely in love, that condition is permanent, lasting a lifetime.* Love, even genuine love, is a fragile thing. It must be maintained and protected if it is to survive. Love can perish when a husband works seven days a week ... when there is no time for romantic activity ... when he and his wife forget how to talk to each other. The keen edge in a loving relationship may be dulled through the routine pressures of living. Where does your marriage rank on your hierarchy of values? Does it get the leftovers and scraps from your busy schedule, or is it something of great worth to be preserved and supported? It can die if left untended.

9. *I believe short courtships (six months or less) are best.* The answer to this question is incorporated in the reply to the second item regarding infatuation. Short courtships require impulsive decisions about lifetime commitments, and that is risky business, at best.

10. *I believe teen-agers are more capable of genuine love than are older people.* If this item were true, then we would be hard pressed to explain why half the teen-age marriages end in divorce in the first five years. To the contrary, the kind of love I have been describing—unselfish, giving, caring, commitment—requires a sizeable dose of maturity to make it work. And maturity is a partial thing in most teen-agers. Adolescent romance is an exciting part of growing up, but it seldom meets the criteria for the deeper relationships of which successful marriages are composed.

Summary

All ten items on this brief questionnaire are false, for they represent the ten most common misconceptions about the meaning of romantic love. I wish the test could be used as a basis for issuing marriage licenses; those scoring 9 or 10 would qualify with honor; those getting 5-8 items right would be required to wait an extra six months before marriage; those dummies answering four or fewer items correctly would be recommended for permanent celibacy. To which groups would you be assigned?

Questions and Answers

Question: I have often wondered why women seem to need romantic involvement so much more than men. Why do you think emotional coolness is a greater agitation to wives than to their husbands?

Answer: An unknown portion of this romantic need in women is probably related to genetic influences implemented by the hypothalamus region in the brain. Beyond this, the characteristic features probably result from differences in early experiences of girls and boys. The entire orientation for little girls in our society is toward romantic excitement. It begins during the preschool years with childhood fantasies, such as Cinderella dazzling the crowd (and particularly the Prince) with her irresistible charm, or Sleeping Beauty being tenderly kissed back to consciousness by the handsome young man of her dreams. While little boys are identifying with football superstars and gun toting cowboys, their sisters are playing "Barbie Dolls" and other role-oriented games which focus on dating and heterosexual relationships. Later, the typical high school girl will spend much more time daydreaming about marriage than will her masculine counterpart. He will think about sex, to be sure, but she will be glassy-eyed over love. She will buy and read the romantic pulp magazines . . . not he! Thus, males and females come to marriage with a lifelong difference in outlook and expectation.

Question: Why, then, are men so uninformed of this common aspect of feminine nature?

Answer: They haven't been told. For centuries, women have been admonished to meet their husbands' sexual needs—or else. Every female alive knows that the masculine appetite for sex demands gratification, one way or the other. What I have been attempting to say is that a woman's need for emotional fulfillment is just as pressing and urgent as the physiological requirement for sexual release in the male. Both can be stymied, but at an enormous cost! And as such, it is as unfortunate for a man to ignore his wife's need for romantic love as it is for her to foreclose on his sexual appetite.

For the benefit of my masculine readers, let me restate my message more directly: your wife is probably more vulnerable to your warmth and kindness than you have realized heretofore. Nothing builds her esteem more effectively than for you to let her (and others) know that you respect and value her as a person. And nothing destroys her self-confidence more quickly than your ridicule or rejection. If you doubt this fact, I urge you to conduct a simple experiment. At the breakfast table tomorrow morning, spontaneously tell your children how fortunate they are to have the mother whom God has given them. Without speaking directly to her, tell them how hard she works to keep them clean and well fed, and then mention how much you appreciate and love her. Just drop these words casually into the middle of your conversation while she is scrambling the eggs. Her reaction will give you valuable insight into her emotional state. If she goes into shock and burns the eggs, then it has definitely been too long since you gave her an unsolicited compliment. If she flashes a mischievous smile and suggests that you miss the 8:05 train this once, you'll then know how to cure the headaches she's been having at bedtime each evening. But if she fails to notice your comments, you must recognize that she is in critical condition and can only be resuscitated by taking her on a weekend trip to a nearby resort, at which time you will have flowers, candy and a love letter waiting in the selected motel.

How long has it been since you *consciously* attempted to convey respect to your wife?

Question: Do most women still want a strong husband who will assume leadership in their home?

Answer: Someone said, "A woman wants a man she can look up to, but one who won't look down on her." That quotation is very old, but it has weathered the Women's Liberation Movement and is still rather accurate. Again, a woman is usually comfortable in following masculine leadership if her man is loving, gentle, and worthy of her respect.

60